IN SEARCH OF SPIRITUALITY

IN SEARCH OF SPIRITUALITY

Finding a way through the spiritual maze

Michael Green

MONARCH
BOOKS

Oxford, UK & Grand Rapids, Michigan, USA

Published by Monarch Books
an imprint of
Lion Hudson plc
Wilkinson House, Jordan Hill Road,
Oxford OX2 8DR, England
Email: monarch@lionhudson.com
www.lionhudson.com/monarch

ISBN: 978-1-85424-802-2

First edition 2007

Acknowledgments
Unless otherwise stated, Scripture quotations are
taken from the New Revised Standard Version Bible, copyright
1989, Division of Christian Education of the National Council of
the Churches of Christ in the United States of America. Used by
permission. All rights reserved.

A catalogue record for this book is available from
the British Library.

Contents

1

How Can I Find a Way Through the Spiritual Maze?

How different it all is from thirty years ago! Those were the days when rationalism ruled OK, when there was little room for spiritual search or expression. Everything was so brutally logical – and boring. Those were the days when the emotional and spiritual side of your nature was given no recognition in the public square, and was often frowned on in private life.

But what a change today! Everyone is looking for a spirituality. Forget the dull and dusty old arguments of the philosophers. Look for what lifts your spirit. Look for what makes you fully alive. Our spirits have too long been in captivity to the goddess Reason – ever since the eighteenth-century Enlightenment, in fact. But now it is perfectly obvious that we do not do the most interesting things in life, like falling in love, on the grounds of reason alone. Feelings come into it. Most of our life is run on feelings – think of Monday morning, or when you score a goal, or have your first deep kiss. Our spirits have too long been in prison. It is time to celebrate our freedom.

And we have been doing that for three decades or more. We currently enjoy a level of material prosperity which most of us have never had before. But the strange thing is that material possessions do not satisfy. I remember a famous musician saying to me, 'I can tell you this, Michael, making a million brings zero satisfaction'. Aristotle Onassis, the world's richest man, died proclaiming, 'Money does not make you happy'.

Everyone is after it, of course. I suppose there has never been such an acquisitive age. But we all know that it does not satisfy. There is that hunger for something more. You find it in the expression, 'There must be more to life than this.' And maybe that is why the spiritual search has taken hold so strongly since the latter part of the twentieth century. Materialism (though we couldn't do without it) is old hat. It doesn't satisfy and it leaves too much of our human experience unexplained.

This new quest for the spiritual takes so many forms. The essence of it is 'Do your own thing.' So you find some people following the example of the Beatles and seeking out some Eastern guru. You find some going in for tantric sex. You find some exploring the ancient wisdom of the Egyptian Pharaohs, or the secrets of Stonehenge. For some, this spirituality means watching the sun set over the Grand Canyon; for others it means getting involved in Wicca or the New Age. Nature mysticism grabs some, while others are obsessed by health foods or fitness regimes.

I doubt whether there has ever been such fascination with exotic religious cults, in the hope that they just might have something to offer. Hinduism has never had such influence in the West as it has today, through transcendental meditation and a multitude of colourful gurus. And new religious movements are mushrooming all over the place. It's not just the Jehovah's Witnesses and the Mormons who come to your door these days. The Hare Krishna crowd may be dancing in the town square, or the Moonies may be selling literature outside the supermarket. And if you take the UFO enthusiasts and the horoscope readers into account as well, it is plain that we are not merely spiritual seekers: we are positively hooked on the supernatural. The gods have come back with a vengeance!

The phenomenal response to *The Da Vinci Code* – a book with more errors in it than raisins in a fruit-cake – is a classic example of the way people today are searching for a spirituality that is exciting, different, non-Christian, morally undemanding, and sensuous. It's a great time to be alive. Nobody is telling you what to do or what to seek. It's up to you.

Yes, indeed it is. But there is just one little problem. How can I find a way through the maze of spiritualities on offer? How can I find something that really works, that satisfies my spirit without rubbishing my mind – something that would work for me and also for society at large? That's the problem.

This book sets out to explain how we can have a spirituality like that. I believe it is to be found in the person who split history in two – Jesus Christ. 'Oh,' I hear you say, 'that's so dated and uncool!' So is food, but it's what we need to keep us healthy. Why not suspend judgment on the Jesus stuff for a moment, and concentrate on what would be needed if we were to find a spirituality that could both satisfy us and also be universally applicable? A spirituality to live by needs to be like that.

A spirituality to live by has got to be true

If you go for a lovely fairytale, it will not support you when disaster strikes, when a lover leaves or when cancer is diagnosed. You will not be able to live with something you know is not true, nor will you be able to pass it on to others with conviction. Deep down inside, you know very well that a spirituality will not pass the test unless it is true, unless it corresponds with the way the world is. I submit to you that Jesus does. He is not merely true. He is the Truth.

A spirituality to live by has got to be relevant

It may be true, but if it does not make any difference in ordinary life, you can keep it, so far as I am concerned. A lot of what passes for Christianity does not seem to make any noticeable difference to the Sunday congregation – or, indeed, to the divorce statistics among professing Christians, for that matter. Church folk seem no happier, no kinder, no more honest, reliable or easy to live with than those who don't go to church. If church on Sundays is all there is to Christianity, you would be wise to look elsewhere for spiritual satisfaction. Mercifully, it isn't!

A spirituality to live by has got to be able to change lives

That's the whole point. If it can't remove fear, especially the fear of death; if it can't break bad habits that have become engrained; if it can't clean guilt up from the conscience, then it is not good enough for the likes of me. You too, I guess. But the really brilliant thing about a relationship with Jesus is this: nobody has ever been too bad for him to take on, and nobody who has ever got into personal touch with him has remained unchanged.

A spirituality to live by has got to offer hope to society at large

If a belief system is merely individual, it is petty. If it is merely social, it is ineffective. Part of the attractiveness of authentic Christian faith is that it has regularly inspired reform, education, medicine, science and idealism in whole nations, as well as transforming individuals. Unlike Communism, it offers the hope of a fulfilment in which all can share, not merely the generation that happens to be alive when the Fulfilment State arrives. Unlike Buddhism, which offers us a future with our individuality rubbed out (since we will all be absorbed into the universal One), Jesus' promise to his people is that they will be with him forever in God the Father's home. Every individual will be there. Everyone will matter. And love, not oblivion, will be the order of the day.

A spirituality to live by has to have a universal appeal

If it is true at all, it must be true for all. Jesus is the man for all races, all seasons – rich and poor, Inuit and Nubian, educated and ignorant. The sheer universality of Christian spirituality is what you would expect if it really *is* the answer to our human quest. And why should we be embarrassed to claim that there is a single answer that meets the needs of all people? It is fashionable to claim that all religions and spiritualities may lead to God, just as all paths can lead up the same mountain. But what if that is a false analogy? What if the world of religions and spiritualities is more like a dark and confusing maze, where there is only one path that leads you out into the sunshine? It's a possibility worth examining.

Anyhow, these are some of the things I would want to look for in a spirituality that has to bear my weight through life and in the face of death. It must be based on truth, not fantasy. It must be relevant, able to change the lives of individuals and society for the better. It must meet the deepest needs of humankind, and it must be applicable to all people everywhere. I don't think you will find anyone else who can offer you a spirituality that fulfils all those conditions. That is why it is worth bothering about Jesus, and not writing him off as old-fashioned and out-of-date. After all, faith in him has been the prevailing spirituality in much of the world for the past 2,000 years. It has affected art, literature, poetry, legislation, medicine and culture more than any other factor or combination of factors. Currently it is out of fashion in the West, but that does not mean it has nothing to offer. As a matter of fact, the Christian faith embraces (notionally, at least!) more than a third of the world's population. Something like 100,000 people turn to Christ every day, worldwide. Never before in history has there been a time of such rapid growth of Christian spirituality! Jesus might just prove to be the way out of the maze.

2

How Can I Be Confident that My Path is Trustworthy?

have been very upfront with you. I have made it quite clear that, in my view, Jesus is the most trustworthy basis for any modern spirituality, as he has been for the last 2,000 years. But that depends, doesn't it, on whether or not Jesus is real. For a great many people, Jesus is not real. He is make-believe, like Cinderella. He is a folk-hero like Robin Hood. Most people learn almost nothing about Jesus at home or at school these days, and their ideas about him may well go back to a few mornings in Sunday School, when they were packed off, protesting, while Mum and Dad read the Sunday papers in bed. Why should anyone believe Jesus is real? Why should anyone dream of basing their spirituality on him and his teaching?

Try asking a mountaineer why he bothers to climb the Matterhorn or Everest. He will probably reply, 'Because it's there.' That is one very good reason for bothering with Jesus. He is there. Look into it and you will find that he was a real historical figure, and not a myth, a legend or some make-believe hero.

The existence of the church shows that Jesus was real

Whatever you may think about it, you can't really ignore a worldwide body of some two billion people who can trace their faith back to a historical figure, Jesus of Nazareth. The first Christians were all Jewish, and their religion sprang from the religion of Israel. The only basic difference was this: the Christians were sure that the great Deliverer for whom Judaism had been waiting had actually come in the person of Jesus of Nazareth. Round about the year AD 30 this new movement called Christianity emerged from Judaism with nothing distinctive about it apart from the unshakeable conviction that the Deliverer had come. He was Jesus. He had died on a cross, and the Christians were confident that, in some mysterious way, this dealt with the guilt of the whole world. More of that anon. They were also convinced that death was not the end of him. He had come alive again: hundreds of them had met him after what they called his resurrection. Anyone could come to know him if they welcomed his Holy Spirit into their hearts and lives. And he was building a new society, the Christian church.

This movement spread fast. Within thirty years there were Christians in all the main cities of the Roman Empire, and an unusual lot they seemed. A mixture of Jews and Greeks, there seemed to be few people of influence among them, and yet their numbers kept growing. They seemed happy, unselfish, very sure that they were forgiven people, and full of love for all and sundry. This really was odd. Probably the 'love' seemed a bit warped. After all, they called each other 'brother' and 'sister', and they were reputed to eat somebody's body and blood. Highly suspicious. So they were just the sort of folk the Emperor Nero could use to take the blame for the Great Fire of Rome (AD 64) – which he probably started himself in order to enlarge his palace grounds! But popular or not, the phenomenal growth of the early church shows that its founder was a real person. It is impossible to explain it otherwise.

The Gospels show that Jesus was real

The Gospels were a completely new form of literature, thrown up by this new movement. There were, of course, links with earlier historical writings, but nobody had ever written Gospels before. There were four of them and they were written by Jesus' followers and their associates. Much of the material had clearly been passed on by word of mouth before it got written down some thirty or forty years after Jesus' death – the ancients preferred the spoken to the written word. The Gospels were, of course, written by different men with differing perspectives, but the figure they bring before us is manifestly the same. All four of them have the spell of Jesus about them. He made such a fantastic impact on them that the normal categories of history and biography did not seem adequate. His followers were impelled to start a completely new literary genre – the Gospel – in order to do justice to this unique person.

Incidentally, in case anybody tells you that the

Gospels have been corrupted and embroidered as the centuries have rolled by, you might be interested to know that the manuscript tradition is far stronger for our Gospels than for any other ancient book. For example, Thucydides, the famous Greek historian, wrote his work about 400 BC, and the earliest manuscript of it that we possess comes from the eleventh century AD. Yet no classical scholar doubts the reliability of the text simply because there was a time gap of about 1,400 years. Or take Tacitus. He was a Roman historian of high calibre who wrote around AD 100. Books 1–6 of his *Annals* come from a single Latin manuscript of the ninth century AD, while books 11–16 come from a single eleventh-century manuscript. Yet nobody doubts that they are authentic and represent what Tacitus wrote. However, because the issues that they raise are so great, people tend to question the reliability of the New Testament documents.

With the Gospels, however, we possess manuscripts which go back to within a hundred years, or less, of the originals, and there are several thousand ancient copies written in more than a score of languages. There are some scribal errors, of course, but we have so many testimonies to the correct text that there is almost always little doubt about it. Certainly, no matter of Christian faith rests on a disputed reading. The text of the New Testament is rock solid. We can be confident that the Gospels have come down to us very much as they were written. They are as real and firm as the Jesus whom they present.

Ancient Roman historians show us that Jesus was real

That is very remarkable when you come to think about it, because those literary Romans were very superior creatures. Why should they bother with a peasant teacher who lived on the very edge of the Roman map, in Judaea? Nevertheless, some of them did bother. Pliny was the governor of Northern Turkey, up by the Black Sea, in about AD 112. He wrote lots of letters to the Emperor Trajan, and they have survived. He tells us about the Christians – their numbers, their influence (the sale of sacrificial animals for the pagan temples had dropped to almost zero), their worship (early in the morning with hymns to Christ as God), their loving and blameless lives, and their regrettable unwillingness to give up their Christian spirituality when he told them to! Many of them he executed, but the movement refused to lie down and roll over. You can read all about it in Pliny's *Letters* (10.96).

Another aristocratic Roman writer was Cornelius Tacitus, the governor of the rich Roman province of Asia Minor (central and coastal Turkey). He tells us that the Emperor Nero picked on the Christians as scapegoats for the Great Fire of AD 64. He writes of the incredible cruelty perpetrated against them: some were clothed in the skins of wild beasts and torn apart by dogs, while others were covered in pitch and set alight at night in Nero's gardens. Tacitus felt sorry for them, but he didn't like them. With well-bred distaste he notes:

> The name 'Christian' comes to them from Christ, who was executed in the reign of Tiberius by the procurator Pontius Pilate. And the pernicious faith, suppressed for a while, broke out afresh and spread not only throughout Judaea, the source of the disease, but even throughout Rome itself, where everything vile comes and is celebrated.   (*Annals* 15.44)

There is plenty of other contemporary Roman evidence that Jesus was a real person. The cities of Herculaneum and Pompeii were overwhelmed by a volcano in AD 79, and Christian mosaics, wall paintings and inscriptions have been found there – also, in all probability, an early Christian chapel. Archaeology has also come up with a decree from the Emperor Tiberius (AD 14–38) or Claudius (AD 41–54) – discovered in Nazareth, of all places! – which threatens the death penalty for anyone who disturbs tombs. It looks as if this may well have been the official reaction to Pontius Pilate's report on the empty tomb of Jesus – nobody in normal circumstances was put to death for robbing a tomb! In short, there can be no doubt in the mind of anyone who takes historical evidence seriously that Jesus actually lived and died in Palestine under the governorship of Pontius Pilate, which ended in AD 36.

The Jewish writers also show that Jesus was real

Christianity soon became a great threat to Judaism, and there is evidence in Jewish documents that the very mention of Jesus was frowned upon. Nevertheless, scattered throughout Jewish writings of the time there are allusions such as: 'Rabbi Eliezer said, "Balaam looked out and saw that there was a man, born of a woman, who would rise up and make himself God, and cause the whole world to go astray."' We read of Jesus' miracles, with the disparaging comment: 'He learnt magic in Egypt.' We read, too, of his death: 'They hanged Jeshua of Nazareth on the eve of Passover.' But the most surprising passage of all is found in the writings of Josephus (*Antiquities* 18.3). He was an influential refugee, writing in Rome in the AD 90s, and he was very keen to keep his nose clean and get the best possible deal for his conquered countrymen, who were still smarting after the sack of Jerusalem by the Romans in AD 70. So you would not expect him to say much about a controversial figure like Jesus. What, then, do you make of this?

> And there arose about this time [i.e. when Pontius Pilate was governor of Judaea, AD 26–36] Jesus, a wise man, if indeed we should call him a man; for he was a doer of marvellous deeds, a teacher of men who receive the truth with pleasure. He won over many Jews, and also many Greeks. This man was the Messiah. When Pilate had condemned him to the cross at the instigation of our leaders, those who had loved him from the first did not cease. For he appeared to them on the third day alive again, as the holy prophets had predicted, and said many other wonderful things about him. And even now the race

of Christians, so named after him, has not yet died out.

When you get a piece as explicit as that from an anti-Christian writer, it's pretty shattering. No wonder lots of people have attacked that text. Nevertheless, this passage is there in all the manuscripts of Josephus. Some of it may well be ironic. But there can be no doubt, from these Jewish references as a whole, that Jesus was a real historical person who made an enormous impression upon his contemporaries. There are allusions, scattered through all this hostile testimony, to his unusual birth ('born of a woman' means 'conceived out of wedlock' in Jewish culture), his date, his disciples, his miracles (although assigned to the devil's agency!), his claims ('made himself God'), his messiahship, his death on a cross, his reported resurrection and his continuing impact on society through his followers. This is a great deal to have gleaned from sources which, for different reasons, were strongly opposed to Christianity.

So wherever you look in the ancient records, be they Christian, archaeological, Roman or Jewish, you find the same message. Jesus was real: we can rely on that. But then, Mohammed and Moses were real, too. Why should anyone turn to Jesus as their spiritual leader? That's a good question. Read on.

3

How Can I Find the Best Spiritual Guide?

have not concealed my conviction that Jesus is the best guide to spirituality. I have shown that he was a real person. But why should we pay any more attention to him than to any of the other great spiritual leaders of humankind? What makes Jesus so special? There are many ways in which Jesus transcends any other great leader who has ever lived. But one is supreme. It is all about who he was ... and who he is.

Jesus of Nazareth is unique in that he claimed that he had come to show us human beings what God is like. He did it not merely by talk but by action. In his own person he brought God before our eyes. The managing director came down to the shop floor. That is the claim. All other great leaders could give their advice: 'This is the way; follow it.' Jesus alone seems to have said: 'I am the way; follow me.'

Jesus lived the simple life of a Jewish working man. He did not own a house. He did not go to college. He did not get married. He became a wandering teacher of spiritual wisdom about God's kingdom, and a bunch of men and women went round with him – that was a common way of learning in antiquity. But despite this humble background, we find him calling God 'Abba', which means 'dear Daddy'. Nobody in all of history before Jesus was ever recorded as speaking about God like that. He even claimed that he had existed before Abraham had been born, about 2,000 years earlier: 'before Abraham was, I am' (John 8:58). He claimed that whoever had seen him had seen the Father (John 14:9). He claimed that he embodied new life after death and could give eternal life to those who entrusted themselves to him (John 11:25ff.). He claimed that nobody could know God as Father except through himself, who had made the Father known (Matthew 11:25–27; John 14:10ff.). He claimed that he had been given the divine right to forgive sins (Mark 2:9–11). He even accepted worship as his due (John 20:28). To cap it all, he maintained that at the end of time the task of judging humankind and separating 'the sheep from the goats' would be entrusted to none other than himself (Matthew 7:22–24; 25:31–46).

Reflect for a moment on the monumental nature of such claims, especially in the passionately monotheistic culture in which Jesus lived. Can you think of any spiritual guide who ever claimed anything so comprehensive? No, claims like these render Jesus absolutely unique among the great leaders of mankind's spiritual search.

But it is all very well to make such claims. How could Jesus have demonstrated them so convincingly that hundreds of millions of people two millennia later remain convinced? A number of factors combined to persuade his first followers. They have remained impressive ever since.

They were impressed by his life

It was matchless. Nobody could point to a single thing wrong with it. For love, courage, self-sacrifice, integrity, prayerfulness, peace and sheer godliness, there has never been anyone who has come near to the standards set by Jesus. Gradually, those living closest to him found themselves reflecting, 'This man has none of the normal human failings. Could he be more than just a man?'

They were impressed by his teaching

It was the most direct and profound teaching that has ever fallen from human lips. Read a Gospel, and judge for yourself. His teaching was so attractive that people went into voluntary unemployment for the privilege of listening to him at length. He claimed that his teaching was not just his own but came from God the Father (John 7:16). It certainly seemed like that to the thousands who crowded to hear him. And so it has seemed to many ever since.

They were impressed by his miracles

Nobody had ever done the things Jesus did. Here were miracles of healing – he healed the blind, the deaf, the crippled, the lepers, and on occasion he is reported to have raised the dead. Here were miracles over nature – the feeding of five thousand from a few bread rolls, the changing of water into wine at a friend's wedding, walking on water in the midst of a massive storm and then instantaneously bringing about a dead calm. Add to those the supreme miracles of his birth and resurrection, and you will see why people were won over. These miracles were done not to show off, but to indicate that in him the long-promised kingly rule of God had arrived. 'Who is this?' they asked. 'Even the winds and waves obey him' (Matthew 8:27).

They were impressed by his fulfilment of prophecy

The Old Testament was full of prophecies about the day when God would personally intervene in the world to rescue his people. They spoke of a king of David's stock whose dominion would be endless, of a prophet like Moses whose teaching would be unparalleled, of a servant of the Lord whose suffering would be intense and who would atone for the sins of all people. They spoke of a 'son' of God whose character would measure up to that of his Father. He would be born in humble circumstances, in a place called Bethlehem. He would both restore Israel and be a light to the non-Jews. He would be rejected by his people and killed, but that would not be the end of him. He would live again and the Lord's purposes would prosper in his hands. All of this came true with Jesus. Not some of it – all of it. It is something totally unique in human history that so many predictions made centuries beforehand should all find their fulfilment in a particular individual. That makes him rather special!

They were impressed by his death

You can see this from the major coverage it gets in the Gospels. It is no mere last chapter to his life – it is the purpose of his life. He came 'to give his life as a ransom for many' (Mark 10:45), a mysterious claim that was not infrequently on his lips. 'Ransom' means to gain back at great cost. Jesus' death was no accident, brought on by jealousy and hostility among religious leaders. Beneath all that there was a purpose – to take responsibility for the waywardness and wickedness of humankind, to pay the price for their release and reinstatement in God's favour. We will be thinking more of that in the next chapter.

They were impressed by his resurrection

Who would not be? Here was the only person in all history who came back from the grave. To be sure, a few, like Lazarus, had been resuscitated for a brief time, but they all had to die in due course. The whole New Testament reverberates with this assured conviction: 'We know that Christ, being raised from the dead, will never die again; death no longer has dominion over him' (Romans 6:9). The resurrection of Jesus from the grave, witnessed by more than 500 people at once

(1 Corinthians 15:6), was the final demonstration, to the first followers of Jesus, that here was no mere man, no brilliant guru, but God himself, who had come to show his hand in the messy affairs of human beings, had with unbelievable generosity paid the price for their evil deeds, and was alive for ever more – alive and available to be met.

Those first Christians electrified the ancient world with this message of a long-expected Messiah, God's own anointed delegate, who had come and died and risen for us all. People need no longer live fruitlessly searching for a reliable spiritual guide. God himself had come searching for people to take him as their guide. And who could be more trustworthy than the ultimate source of our being, the living God himself?

4

How Can I Start the Journey?

I t is one thing to recommend Jesus Christ as the best and most reliable guide to the things of the spirit, but you may rightly wonder precisely what he offers. To give an adequate answer would be like trying to capture the ocean in a cockleshell. But here are three aspects of what he offers which I do not think you will find available from any other source. Other spiritual guides can offer comfort, purpose in life, peace and some measure of fulfilment. None can offer these three.

First, he offers *cleansing* from whatever has defiled us in the past. We do not think about our wrongdoings very much these days. It is not cool. Ours is a society where everyone does their own thing and nobody (except judges!) sits in judgment on the lifestyle of others. But a moment's reflection will show how shallow this assumption is. You cannot get away from the fundamental difference between right and wrong, however hard you try. You cannot pretend that racism, paedophilia, violence, murder and fraud are acceptable.

They are not. They are destructive of personality and community. They are also destructive of our relationship with God, the supreme Spirit. God must surely be pure perfection, or he would not be God. If he is pure, how can he accept someone like me who is far from pure? Our words, deeds, thoughts and attitudes have all been corrupted to a greater or lesser extent. That is what the Bible means when it asserts that 'there is no difference: for all have sinned and come short of the glory of God' (Romans 3:23). Of course, there are lots of differences between us. But there is no difference in this respect: we have all done wrong, repeatedly, and we all fall short of God's standard for human life. We can see what that is like when we look at the life of Jesus. Measured against that quality of life, we do not even begin to compete! Inevitably that poses a problem. How can a pure and perfect God have dealings with impure and imperfect human beings? That is a problem as old as time itself. People have wrestled with it in countless ways: sacrifices, confessions, hair shirts, the lot. But none of it is effective, because the trouble is not what we *do* so much as what we *are* – imperfect, to put it mildly! The glory of the Christian good news – and it is very good news indeed – is that God realized that we could never make it on our own. So he, the Judge, came to stand in the dock alongside us, the guilty ones; and even more, he was willing to accept the penalty that our wrongdoings and failings had incurred.

And what was that penalty? In a word, alienation. That is what we get when we turn our backs on God and are determined to have our own way and do our own thing. That inevitably causes a rift between us and God. Well, God was determined to bridge that rift, whatever it cost. And it cost him Calvary. You may rightly ask why that particularly grisly form of death should be so significant. Because at the heart of the crucifixion we see not only the bestial brutality of men, but the desolating alienation of the patient sufferer, who cried out, 'My God, my God, why have you forsaken me?' Jesus underwent the separation from God, the total alienation from all that is good, on our behalf on that cross, so that we should never have to live with the consequences of our failures and rebellions. That's how much God loves us!

But how could the death of one person, however good, atone for a whole world's guilt? The point is that he was not just one man. He was the God-man, as we saw in the previous chapter. As man, he stood in for human beings at the point of their greatest need. As God, what he did on the cross has lasting consequences and need never be repeated. So Jesus can offer all who come to him not just forgiveness but a whole new standing with God, a clean sheet. It is perfectly just, since he has himself paid our debt. It is perfectly loving, because that is what God is like! Nowhere else, in the religions and philosophies of the world, will you find a loving, intellectually satisfying offer of cleansing from all your failures. It is utterly unique, and it is profoundly life-changing.

The second thing that Jesus uniquely offers us is his *companionship* at all times. No mere guru can do that. We cannot be in their company continually. But that is where the resurrection of Jesus is so relevant. Although he died on Good Friday, he rose back to unquenchable life on the first Easter Day.

The first disciples could hardly believe it, but we have five accounts in the New Testament of how they became persuaded that their Jesus was not lost for good and all, but was alive and relevant to their situation. He showed himself to some of them in a house, on a walk, on a fishing trip, at breakfast and so on. He was proving to them that he was alive and available, and could be their constant companion, once he had left this world physically so that he could return unencumbered by the limitations of a physical body, and become the unseen spiritual guide and companion to whoever would welcome him.

All that had convinced the disciples that Jesus was alive again. But six weeks after the crucifixion, on the great festival of Pentecost, he made himself known in a new and lasting way – by the gift of his Spirit. His amazed followers found that Jesus was no mere historical figure but that, in some mysterious way, he actually came to be present in their lives. I do not think you will find anywhere else a spiritual guide who offers you lasting and unbroken companionship like that. Armed with this assurance of his unfailing companionship, they set out to win the ancient world for Christ. And to a remarkable extent they succeeded. Within a generation they had spread throughout the Middle East, into France, Germany and Spain, as far as Britain in the west, into India in the east, and deep into Africa in the south. This was a staggering achievement for a group of passionate enthusiasts who had discovered the best news in the world and were determined to spread it.

Thirdly, Jesus tells his followers that we matter so much to God that God will not scrap us at the end of our lives but will *take us home with him* – for ever. That is what heaven is all about: being with the Lord who loves us, for ever. This may sound like 'pie in the sky when we die', but that would be too shallow an assessment. The well-attested resurrection of Jesus from the grave is the first instalment of what he offers to all his people. It is solid evidence that death is not the end, but is the doorway to a fuller life shared with the God who gave it. I do not think you will find any other spiritual guide who makes a comparable offer – or if they do, none of them can back the credibility of their offer with evidence as rock solid as the resurrection of Jesus Christ.

Yes, Jesus offers us cleansing, companionship and eternal life. He offers them as a free gift – we do not have to spend ages working for them. 'The gift of God is eternal life', the Bible insists. It is a gift: we could never earn it. But how do we receive this amazing offer?

There has to be an act of will on our part, a declaration of intent to make this Jesus our spiritual leader. We have to join up. You cannot become a member of a business organization, or of the armed forces, or indeed of a marriage, without signing on. That is exactly what you do if you want to start the journey of life with Jesus Christ. You quite deliberately sign on. You tell him that you are sorry you have made a mess of things hitherto, going down all sorts of roads that turned out to be dead ends. You tell him that you want to start travelling with him on your journey, both now and for the rest of your life. You tell him you will be glad to accept his leadership, even when that is hard. And then you sign on. Quite decisively. You ask him to come with his unseen Spirit to become your companion along the road.

That's where it all starts. And it is a beginning that we cannot duck out of if we want Jesus to be our spiritual guide. It is humbling – to admit we have not been on the right road. It is costly – to allow him to call the shots in future. It is embarrassing – to be known as his friends. But it is the start of the most satisfying relationship in the world. Don't miss out on it. Ask him to take you on. Starting this relationship is so simple that many miss it. It begins with a simple act of commitment to Jesus and his cause, and an honest request for him to put his unseen but very real Spirit into us.

Last night six people who had been meeting for a few evenings in my house, told me (and each other) that they had taken this step, and there was much rejoicing! They had started the most exciting and fulfilling adventure open to humankind. Of course, that is only the beginning of our journey with Jesus, which will last until the end of our lives and into the life to come. But it is an indispensable beginning. You cannot be a soldier without signing on. You cannot be a Christian without signing on with Christ.

You might like to pause now, if you know you have never made that act of surrender, and pray in your own words, but somewhat along these lines:

Lord, I am sorry I have made a mess of so many things in my life. I am ashamed of my pride and self-centredness and all the other things that must grieve you. I am willing for you to make the changes I cannot manage on my own.

I am so grateful that in your love, you came to find me, and that you went to the cross in order to take responsibility for all the bad stuff in my life. I am grateful, too, that you are the Easter Jesus. I believe you rose from the grave and are alive and willing to accept me into your family.

I realize it will be costly to follow you as my leader and boss. I think I am prepared for that.

So here and now, I want to sign on. I want to start travelling down the road in your company. I want to commit as much of myself as I can understand to as much of you as I can understand. I want to invite your unseen Holy Spirit to come into my life. I want to be some use to you during the remainder of my life.

Lord, here I am. Please take me on and then send me out to be one of your representatives.

God never turns a deaf ear to a prayer like that.

5

How Can I Be Sure Where I Stand?

think I hear you saying, 'It can't be as simple as that! It's one thing to pray and ask Jesus to be my spiritual guide and leader, but quite another to be sure that he has heard, or that he will take any notice of me. How can I be sure I am welcomed?'

Good question. Some people never get it sorted. And so they go through life hoping they are followers of Jesus, trying to be, but quite unsure whether they belong or not. When you stop to think about it, that is a very unsatisfactory position to stay in: I know I am a Brit. I know I am married. I know I am an Anglican. But I am not sure whether I am a Christian! That is the place where a lot of people are at. But it's crazy, all the same. The good news is that we are not meant to stay there.

If this relationship with Jesus were the result of our own achievements, I could understand the hesitation that many people feel about declaring themselves Christians. They (rightly) doubt if they are good enough to earn the title. But the Bible makes it very plain that we are not accepted because of our achievements but because God himself came in the person of Jesus Christ to rescue us. 'The gift of God is eternal life', we are told (Romans 6:23). If I give you a gift at Christmas, I expect you to know that you have got it. You don't insult me by trying to pay for it. You don't get big-headed about it, as though it was some virtue of your own that produced it. You simply take it and say 'Thank you.' It is like that with God. He gives us the Holy Spirit of Jesus to be our guide and companion. He expects us to receive the gift with awe and wonder and to say 'Thank you.'

This 'Holy Spirit', (as the New Testament calls the Spirit of Jesus who comes to accompany us through life), is not slow to show his hand. It's like those notices you sometimes see in a shop or restaurant: 'This business is under entirely new management.' Of course, it does not all become obvious at once. There are considerable repairs and renovations to be done, and it takes time. It's just the same in the spiritual life. But here are some of the ways the new Companion makes himself known. The First Letter of John, near the end of the New Testament, is full of them.

For one thing, we begin to find growing in us a new desire to please God. In the past I did not care in the least what God wanted me to do. I was out to please myself. But now I want to please the one who loves me, died for me and has come to be my guide (1 John 2:5–6). I don't always succeed. But that is my aim.

Another thing is, I discover in myself a new attitude to other people. It might start with forgiving someone against whom I have long held a grudge. It might mean a new attitude to people in need. In the past I may sometimes have given money away when I felt like it. But now I have to agree with St John, who says: 'If anyone has material possessions and sees his brother in need, but has no pity on him, how can the love of God be in him?' I have no answer to that question – have you? The generous meeting of need in other people is a mark of new life (1 John 3:10, 17). Indeed, if all Christians withdrew from voluntary service to the needy, the social services would collapse!

Another sign that the Spirit has come into residence is love for fellow Christians. Speaking personally, I used to think the 'God squad' was a dull bunch of grey people – before I joined them. Then I discovered an entirely new relationship with them. 'We know that we have passed from death to life, because we love brother Christians', as the apostle John put it (1 John 3:14). It really surprised me. They became my brothers and sisters in the Christian family. Many of them in due course became my best friends. I wanted to be in their company. Not surprising, really – even in nature, birds of a feather flock together.

There is a new power over bad habits, too, that begins to make itself known. 'Greater is he who is in you than he who is in the world', says the old apostle (1 John 4:4). He means you have a power in you now that is greater than the forces pulling you in the wrong direction. When you hold in your hand the book you are now reading, there is the power of gravity pulling it down, but a greater power of life in your hand holding it up.

Remove your hand – and the book falls. Grip it in your hand – and it overcomes the pull of gravity. That is the sort of thing John is trying to explain. Of course, you need to call on that power, but it is there, waiting to be used. And you will experience a liberation from whatever your own addictions may be. In my case it was violence and foul language. The Holy Spirit within us can turn anger into graciousness, or 'beer into furniture', as the Salvation Army put it. And that is something brand new. You can prove it for yourself the very day you invite the Spirit of the Lord to come to you (1 John 3:6; 4:4), though becoming more like Jesus will take rather longer!

Not surprisingly, there is a new joy and confidence around as well. Not that you won't have to go through times of pain and suffering. You will. But there is an underlying joy which comes from the Spirit. John wrote his letter partly in order to draw attention to this exciting change: 'We write this to make your joy complete' (1 John 1:3–4).

There is also something else that many will find very new. It is the experience of answered prayer. Prayer – if you did it at all – is no longer talking to yourself, no longer a ritual to which you have long ceased to expect an answer. When Jesus died on the cross, he broke the sound barrier between us and God. Prayer begins to become companionship with the God who gave us life. The glass ceiling between us and him is smashed. 'This is the confidence that we have in him, that if we ask anything according to his will, he hears us. And if we know that he hears us – whatever we ask – we know that we have what we asked of him' (1 John 5:14–15). We do not always get what we ask for, of course, any more than our kids do when they ask us for things. But we do have the assurance of being heard. And that is wonderful.

Last but not least, there is a new sense of pardon. A wonderful sense that we can get cleaned up. Of course, we all blow it regularly, and Christians are acutely aware of this. But listen to the apostle John: 'If anybody does sin, we have one who speaks to the Father in our defence – Jesus Christ the righteous one. He is the atoning sacrifice for our sins' (1 John 2:2). He paid the price once and for all on the cross. It never needs to be paid again. But we do need to come back and say 'Sorry' and claim afresh that forgiveness which he loves to give us, and which he can quite justly proffer because he has himself done all that is necessary to put us in the right with God. That is the glory of the cross.

Well, there you have it. Those are seven ways in which the Spirit assures us that he has turned up (there are other signs in this little letter: see if you can find them!). 'We know that he abides in us, by the Spirit which he has given us', says St John (1 John 3:24). You will probably not find those signs of new life all emerging at the same time. It is rather as if you were to plant several different kinds of bulbs in your garden in the autumn. They germinate, but they come up at different times: first the snowdrops, then the daffodils, then the hyacinths, then the tulips. It is like that in the garden of your life. The Spirit will produce one or two evidences of germination fairly early on in your spiritual journey, and other marks of the new life will follow in due course.

John sums it up in a lovely way (1 John 5:10–12). He says, in effect, 'If you believe someone when he gives you his word on a matter, how much more can you believe God?' And this is what God has said: 'He has given us eternal life, and this life is in his Son. He who has the Son has life, and he who does not have the Son does not have life.' Simple and clear, is it not? God gives you his word that if you have welcomed the Son, Jesus, to be your spiritual guide and companion, then you share the divine life. If you have him and he has you, you *have* spiritual life. Not 'will have': you *have* the first instalment here and now of a life that will never end. God guarantees it. You see, his eternal life is all wrapped up in Jesus. If you have Jesus, you already have a life with God that will last for ever. Not surprisingly, then, John concludes: 'I write this to you who believe in the name of the Son of God so that you may know that you have eternal life' (1 John 5:13). Do you know it? You are meant to. Take it. Be confident about it. And say a big 'Thank you!'

6

How Can I Grow My Spirituality? (1) The Map

How can we grow our spirituality? There's a good question. And it is such an important one that we shall need to look at it in the next four chapters. We have been provided with a map for the road ahead, a cell phone for instant communication, food for the journey, and the companionship of fellow-travellers. All these things are important if we are to grow spiritually. Let's start with the map.

What is this map?

The spiritual map that God has given us is the Bible. It is a book of ancient wisdom – indeed, it is more a library than a single volume. For it is a collection of some sixty-six books, written by forty or more authors in three ancient languages over a period of a thousand years. It comprises a rich variety of literature – poetry, history, narrative, biography, wisdom literature, straight instruction, letters, apocalypse, and an entirely new literary genre, the gospels. You might think that with such variety, indeed disparity, in its composition, there would be little to justify our calling it a single book. But to our surprise, we find there is a remarkable unity running through its contents. We find just one understanding of God throughout the Bible: he is holy love. We find just one evaluation of humankind: we are made in God's image but marred by self-centredness and in need of restoration. We find just one understanding of true spirituality: the movement is from God to us (in his generous love), not vice versa. There is just one idea of how people, flawed though we all are, can get right with God: it is due to his action in history on our behalf. Throughout the Bible we learn that God wants peace and justice in the world, he wants integrity and love to flourish among human beings, and he wants us to seek after him and find him. And the whole Bible is clear that a future awaits God's people after death – to know God and enjoy him for ever.

You might expect there to be as many different views on such topics as there are authors in the Bible, but no. There is total agreement. How come? Ah, now that's the secret that so many people just don't get. The unity that runs through all the diversity in the Bible derives from its source. And that source is God's own superintendence and inspiration of the human authors. 'All scripture is inspired by God and is useful for teaching, for reproof, for correction and for training in righteousness, so that everyone who belongs to God may be proficient, equipped for every good work' (2 Timothy 3:16). It is 'useful' because it is 'inspired by God'. The apostle

Peter put it like this: 'Men and women moved by the Holy Spirit spoke from God' (2 Peter 1:21). Men and women spoke – in all the diversity of their personal and cultural background. Some of the writers were sophisticated, some simple. Some wrote in polished Greek, some in the Greek of the streets. But God spoke through them all. There is a dual authorship to this book. That is why the Bible is such a reliable map along the path of the spirit. It is derived ultimately from God himself, working in and through a wide variety of human writers.

Why should we consult this map?

In the Bible's own pages we find it described in a number of ways that answer this question. It is a mirror which enables us to see the dirt on our face and do something about it (James 1:22–25). It is a sword that hacks away at our bad habits (Ephesians 6:17). It is a fire to warm us, and a hammer to break down the rock of our resistance (Jeremiah 23:29). It is like milk to nourish the newborn baby (1 Peter 2:2) or meat to feed the more mature (Hebrews 5:14). All these are good reasons for paying attention to this remarkable book. For there is a great deal it can do for us – far more than any map! It has a way of cleansing us from things that may have dirtied us (Psalm 119:9). It certainly offers guidance and direction for us as we try to make progress (Psalm 119:105). It gives a sense of peace and balance in our lives (Proverbs 4:4–6), and above all, it keeps us in touch with our spiritual guide, Jesus himself (John 15:7). In a word, if we want to grow, regular encounter with the Bible is indispensable.

How do we map-read?

There are a few practical things we need to pay attention to. We need to find a place and a time where we will be undisturbed for a short while. We need to get a modern translation of the Bible. We need to make a regular daily time for it. Don't start at Genesis, or you will come to a grinding halt by the time you hit Leviticus! You might like to start with one of the Gospels, followed by the Acts, to see how the early Christians set out to follow Jesus. And then read one of the letters, like Philippians, written to help the first Christians in their spiritual lives.

But you would be wise, especially to begin with, to enlist some help. That is precisely what Bible-reading systems like the Scripture Union, or the Bible Reading Fellowship, exist for. They both offer us a passage of a dozen or so verses each day, with some useful comments and a thought for the day to take with us.

Begin by collecting your thoughts and asking God's Spirit to make something from the day's reading really come alive to you, as if someone switched on a light-bulb. Read it through, slowly. Discover and reflect on the main point of the passage. Then read it again, more slowly! You would be wise to ask yourself what it meant to the original readers, and therefore what it can legitimately mean for you. If you don't ask the first question, you may read all sorts of subjective rubbish into the text. If you don't ask the second question, you will find yourself in a desert of dry information that does nothing for your spiritual life. You would do well to acquire a suitable reference book on the Bible, such as *The Lion Handbook to the Bible* or the *New International Version Study Bible*. They are not a substitute for your own efforts to draw nourishment from the text, but they do make an awful lot of things plain!

As you read the passage slowly and thoughtfully, there are a number of things to look out for. See if you can find some promise that you could claim for yourself. Is there a command that you should obey? You may get some new insight into God or yourself. You may well find an example to follow – or avoid! Perhaps there is a warning to heed, or a prayer to echo. You won't find all of these each time, but you will find some of them. And you will be getting into the habit of asking questions of the text and letting it speak to you.

Very well – now turn what you have found into a short prayer or give thanks for it. Interiorize it, so to speak – meditate on it. Remember that reading the Bible like this is not merely an attempt to gain information. It is all about enhancing relationship. You should be looking for a two-way conversation; God certainly is. He wants you not only to consult the map but to relate to the one who made the map. So get into the habit of praying over what you have read, praying it into your heart and life. And then, go out and do it. It is no good consulting the map and then going off in the opposite direction. The map is a guide for the road. It is meant to lead to progress – including a change of direction, if need be!

7

How Can I Grow My Spirituality? (2) The Cell Phone

Almost everybody these days seems to have a cell phone. It is unobtrusive – indeed, it is usually invisible, hidden deep in a pocket or a purse. Yet it is an invaluable way of keeping in touch with friends we cannot see. We can just call them up to have a chat, to thank them for a gift, or to ask for some help. Instant communication!

Prayer is the cell phone of the spiritual life. It is the unobtrusive, hidden communication between you and God. It is impossible to overstate its importance for the growth of your spirituality.

What opportunities does my cell phone open up?

Just as there is a whole variety of uses you can find for your cell phone, so there is for prayer. It is certainly not just a matter of taking a shopping list to God after you have tried all other avenues in vain!

Prayer includes *worship*. This means revelling in the wonder, greatness and generosity of God. Worship means 'worth-ship', in which we tell God he is worth everything we can offer. It is rather like the old marriage service where the groom promises to 'worship' his bride – to say to her, 'You're worth it!' That both thrills her heart, and puts him in his place. 'Ascribe to the Lord the glory due to his name', cries the psalmist (Psalm 96:8).

Prayer includes *confession*, getting rid of the daily muck we accumulate on the journey through life. Jesus told his followers that once they had come to him and had a complete bath, they would only need to have their feet washed when they got dirty on the dusty Eastern roads (John 13:10). So we do not have to start all over again with God when we mess up. 'If we confess our sins, he who is faithful and just will forgive us our sins and cleanse us from all unrighteousness' (1 John 1:9). 'Faithful' because we are in the family, and 'just' because he has himself paid the price. But it is our responsibility to confess our faults. Otherwise the phone line will go dead, not because our Father has finished the call, but because we can no longer receive the signal.

Prayer involves *thanksgiving*. We do not want to be like ungrateful children, always asking for another present and rarely coming to say 'Thank you.' Anyhow, the more we get into the habit of thanksgiving, the more we will recognize that a good many of our prayers have been or are being answered.

Prayer includes *meditation*, reflecting on Scripture and on how God is at work in our lives. 'I will meditate on your teaching', said the psalmist (Psalm 119:48), but we are in such a rush in today's hectic round of activities that we rarely make time to meditate and allow God's truth to seep into us. That is a big mistake. Meditation allows space for our souls to grow.

Prayer involves *intercession* for other people. Yes, asking is a part of prayer, but if we do it at all, we probably mainly ask for ourselves. Prayer for others is one of the greatest services we can render them. You might like to make a list of people dear to you whom you want to pray for on a regular basis, while leaving room for other folk you may run into who also need your prayers.

Prayer involves *offering ourselves* to serve the Lord, making ourselves available to him. In Romans 12:1 the apostle tells us that spiritual worship means offering God our bodies for him to work through. That would include the way we do our daily work, the proportion of our money we give away, and the way we relate to other people.

And prayer means *listening* as well. Any relationship where only one person speaks is sterile. The Holy Spirit is given to us to prompt prayer within our hearts, and to open up that two-way communication which a good phone call facilitates (Romans 8:26). I find listening to God difficult. As in a phone call, I often miss what the other person is saying because I continue speaking myself! But all the deeply spiritual people I know have taken pains to develop the art of quietly listening to the Guide as well as speaking to him. I'm working on it!

How can I learn to use my cell phone?

Well, practice makes perfect. We learn most by doing it. And just as you can use your cell phone for a regular call or for an occasional conversation, so it is with prayer. Like Daniel, busy prime minister though he was, we need to make a regular time to pray: he did it three times each day (Daniel 6:10). But we also will often want to turn to the Lord when something has gone well or when a problem has arisen. No need to kneel or shut your eyes – though these can help. Just lift your heart to him.

Jesus' friend Peter was trying to follow Jesus in walking on water. Not surprisingly, he failed and began to sink, and at once called out for help. 'Immediately', we read, 'Jesus reached out his hand and caught him' (Matthew 14:31). He will be just as prompt in answering our hurried prayers.

A second way to learn to get comfortable in using the cell phone is to take lessons from Jesus himself. We can learn the Lord's Prayer by heart and often use it. We can also use each phrase of it as a springboard for our own prayers. We could also learn a great deal by meditating on Jesus at prayer in that amazing passage in John 17 when he poured out his heart to the heavenly Father on the last night of his life. In any area of life, examples are such a help. And in this matter of prayer Jesus has given us both a pattern and an example.

There's a third way, too. We can turn to the prayer and praise book of the Bible itself – the Psalms. All human experience is there: cries for help, joy, discouragement, anger, thankfulness – and pervading it all, a deep trust in God. Whatever our mood, we will often find that the Psalms express just what we want to say. Books of prayers can be helpful too, especially if they are the great prayers that believers have used down the centuries. If yours is one of the liturgical churches, it will have a Prayer Book, and there will be some good confessions, prayers and thanksgivings in that. But most of all, we learn from the Holy Spirit himself, who loves to teach his people to use that phone of prayer.

What if there is no reply?

That is quite a common experience in the spiritual life, as well as in the human phone system. 'Sorry, the phone's off the hook ... wrong number ... no reply.' There could be several reasons for the experience of unanswered prayer. It may be that there is unforgiven sin blocking the way: 'If I regard iniquity in my heart, the Lord will not hear me' (Psalm 66:18). It may be that we have not actually prayed about the issue at all (James 4:2). It may be that we have not been serious about our prayer (Matthew 7:7). It may be that we need to learn perseverance in prayer (Luke 18:1–8). It may be that we were selfish in what we were praying for (James 4:3), or that we were not really looking for God's will to be done, but for our own (Mark 14:36). We need to keep in close touch with him, like a branch in a tree (John 15:5–7), if we want that sense of intimacy with him to be retained, and our payers to be answered.

Never forget that answers may not always come in

the form we expect. Sometimes God delays them for our good or for some purpose of his own that we know nothing about. Sometimes we may be meant to answer our own prayer: on one occasion the disciples were told to pray that God would thrust forth labourers into the harvest field – and then Jesus sent them out themselves (Matthew 9:38; 10:5)! God is not an answering machine. He is a person and longs for us to share our lives with him, whatever the answer. We could do worse than learn a lesson from traffic lights. First we need to come to a stop and look for an answer. It may be red, indicating a 'No'. It may be green, saying 'Yes'. But it may be amber, meaning 'Wait'.

For some months I had been praying about a big decision, and could get no indication from God about it. Then suddenly a phone call out of the blue only yesterday showed me the answer with startling clarity. It opened the door to an opportunity far more significant than I could have dreamed of, and one that would not have been available had I got an immediate answer to my prayer!

Our Guide himself reminds us of our need to keep on praying, and not to lose heart (Luke 18:1)!

8

How Can I Grow My Spirituality? (3) The Meal

You can't go far on a journey without getting hungry. And God has provided for his family a marvellous meal as they travel. It has proved so satisfying that it has scarcely changed its ingredients for 2,000 years.

I remember how shocked I was when I discovered in some survey or other that in many homes nowadays the family never has a meal together. They are in and out, each doing their own thing, caught up in the frenetic pace of modern life. But of course, the family can't have much in the way of togetherness or shared experience if they never meet over a meal. In the East, a meal is the supreme mark of belonging, and even in our fragmented Western society, a shared meal is one of the joys of life and a great way of deepening relationships.

The good Lord knows that very well. So he has given us one or two very solid and physical marks of belonging to his family. At the start of the journey he gave us baptism, a graphic sign of the death of the old self-centred life, and the start of a new life shared with him.

And as we continue the journey, he gives us what Christians call the Lord's Supper or the Holy Communion or the Eucharist or the Mass, to speed us on our way. The first of those names means that it is a *meal* we are celebrating; the second stresses that it is *shared* with each other and with him; the third draws attention to the note of joy and *gratitude*; and the fourth name is obscure, but seems to come from the Latin *missa est* – the church, nourished by the meal, is *sent* out into society afresh.

This family meal originated with Jesus himself, and he told his followers to do it in remembrance of him. Very early on, it seems to have become a weekly time of celebration for the Christians. They would gather after work, have an evening together in a home, share news over the meal, encourage one another, pull out of the church box a letter from one of the apostles, like St Paul, and read it to those present. The evening would end with sharing in a common loaf and drinking from a common cup to recall Jesus' presence.

It all goes back to Jesus' Last Supper with his friends. It was not only the night of his arrest: it was Passover time. Passover was the age-old festival of the Jews to celebrate their national deliverance from Egypt, where they had been subjected to slavery and often death. On the night of their deliverance they obeyed God's command, daubed the blood of a lamb on the doorposts of their homes, and started on the long march to freedom.

The Lord told them to keep this night as a permanent reminder of their deliverance. They have done so ever since. Each year they celebrated the Passover, when

God's judgment 'passed over' every house that was painted with the blood. Every year they told the story of their rescue. And it was all so vivid and personal that the president of the feast would say, 'This the Almighty did for *me* when I came out of Egypt.'

Imagine the awed amazement of Jesus' friends when, instead of saying the traditional words, 'This is the bread of affliction which our fathers ate in the wilderness' as he broke the loaf, he said, 'This is my body, which is given for you.' By replacing the traditional formula with his never-to-be-forgotten words, Jesus meant them to see his death as the great deliverance which the slaughter of the Passover lambs had anticipated. His death would secure for them rescue from a worse fate than there had ever been in Egypt: it would mean rescue from the grip of evil in their lives and the death or separation from God which that brought. This was the true liberation to which the Old Testament had pointed forward. And the very next day it all began to come true, as Jesus died on the cross – the Passover Lamb who fulfilled all the Old Testament predictions.

So if we want to understand this special meal which Jesus has left us as food for the journey, we need to glance back at the old Jewish Passover which it replaces. First, like the Passover, the meal looks back to a sacrifice – the sacrifice of Christ on the cross. It was there that he made possible our release. It was there that he dealt with human guilt by assuming personal responsibility for it. So we should come to that meal with a real sense of the wrong we have done and what it cost Jesus to put us right with God. There should be a deep sense of gratitude to the Saviour for his profound love which led him to make such a sacrifice.

Secondly, the Communion is a meal to strengthen us for our journey, as the Passover strengthened the Jews for theirs. Just as our bodies are strengthened by our meals, so our spiritual lives are fed by the bread and wine which symbolize and make available for us the flesh and blood of Jesus – his very self given for us personally. That is the deep mystery of this wonderful meal. He feeds us with himself so that we can go out and represent him in the world.

Thirdly, there has always been a looking forward in the Communion, just as there was in the Passover meal. The old rabbis had a saying: 'On this night they were saved, and on this night they will be saved.' The Passover was a foretaste of the feast of salvation in God's future, just as surely as it was a memorial of God's deliverance in the past. So strongly was this emphasized that each Jewish family would leave an empty chair at the Passover meal, in case Elijah, that great prophet of the last days, should return! And the same looking forward marks the Communion. As St Paul put it, 'We proclaim the Lord's death until he comes' (1 Corinthians 11:26). Just as the Passover was the promise of the Messiah's coming, so the Communion is the pledge of his return at the end of all history. That is why the old Aramaic word *Maranatha* was used at the Communion in the ancient church. It means 'O Lord, come!' At every Communion Christians turn their eyes to heaven, in anticipation of the final feast with their beloved Lord and his people for ever.

Fourthly, it is a meal we share together. Nobody has the Communion on their own. In many churches there is a sharing of the peace, as members embrace each other and leave behind any niggles they may have about other people. This helps to deepen the unity among us and to support us in our common life.

What a wonderful family meal this is! It spells rescue from our accusing past, strength for the daily round, companionship along the road, and a foretaste of heaven. No wonder the Christian family loves to celebrate it often. It embodies the very heart of our spirituality.

9

How Can I Grow My Spirituality? (4) The Companions

Have you noticed how, if you are on a walk, it seems much shorter and much more enjoyable if you are going along with a bunch of friends? Even if your journey is in a car, it is much more interesting if the car is full. Well, it is like that in the spiritual journey that we have been thinking about. It is not a path from the alone to the Alone. It involves companions along the way. It is an accompanied journey. I am grateful that it is.

We must be clear, then, that Christian spirituality is not an isolated affair, but a matter of belonging with others in God's counter-cultural society, the church. Now, I have a shrewd suspicion that the word 'church' may turn you off. It does that to many people. Sometimes it conjures up images of a hierarchical and unbending society. Sometimes it prompts memories of a cold, forbidding building. Sometimes there are echoes of rival denominations at each other's throats. Sometimes it raises memories of some hurt inflicted by 'the church' or one of its representatives. Try to put pictures like that out of your mind. The devil loves to get hold of some words, and 'church' is one of them! The church is not a hierarchy. The church is not a building. The church is not a denomination. And the church is not an organization designed to hurt people.

Who are these companions on the journey?

Jesus just called them 'disciples' or learners. He referred to them in an affectionate turn of phrase as 'a little flock'. The first Christians called themselves 'followers of the Way', which underlines the journey motif we have been considering throughout this book. But the really interesting thing is that the images that the New Testament writers use are always plural. They are not interested in a solitary spirituality. They insist that it has to be corporate. Here are some of the ways in which they describe the church.

Christians are 'the family of God' (Ephesians 2:17–19). As in any family, there are lots of differences between them, but they are bound together into a unity which transcends the differences.

They are 'the temple of the Spirit' (Ephesians 2:19–22; 1 Corinthians 3:16). And that is not merely a metaphor for the Spirit living in the gathered Christian community, but a reminder that each of us is a brick in the building. Each of us is needed. Each is valuable.

They are called 'the body of Christ' (Ephesians 4:15–16). The apostle Paul is particularly fond of this picture – he comes back to it time and again in his letters. He points out how, although the different limbs have different functions, they all belong in the same body and operate under the direction of the same brain.

There are other images as well. Christians are in some sense 'the army of God' (Ephesians 6:10–20). They are 'branches' in Christ, who is seen as the Vine (John 15:1ff.). They are 'athletes' in 'the games' (1 Corinthians 9:24ff.). A very mixed bunch of images, but you will notice that they are all corporate. We belong together. We need each other. And God has given us each other as companions on the road, not to compete with one another but to complement and encourage one another.

Our unity really does matter. Jesus made that the subject of his famous prayer on the last night of his earthly life (John 17:20ff.), and the first Christians managed it, more or less. But it due course human frailty and rival emphases led to the rise of denominations. These are the scandal of the church. God hates divisions in his people. Despite all appearances, there is a God-given unity among all the companions of Jesus on the journey. The apostle Paul spells out some of the links that bind us together. There is one body, in which we are all limbs. There is one Holy Spirit, which all true Christians have received. There is one hope to encourage us all to persevere to journey's end. There is one Lord Jesus whom we seek to follow. There is one trust in him which all share. There is one baptism which we have all received, and there is one mighty God who is above us all, works in us all, and achieves his purposes through us all (Ephesians 4:4–6). These are seven remarkable marks of the unity that God has already given us. We can't make unity. He gives it. But it is our responsibility to try to preserve that unity, and to try to regain it when it is broken. Apart from anything else, the scoffing world is not likely to be attracted to a divided Christian community.

What are they for?

I know what a knife is for. I know what a car is for. But what on earth is the church for? That question is not so unanswerable as it might at first sight appear. The New Testament shows us three main purposes which these journey-companions of Jesus are meant to fulfil.

First, they exist to worship God. To praise and glorify the one who gave us birth – and new birth. To take people out of themselves by revelling in one who is far greater than we are. That is our responsibility to God. Of course it is – we are his creatures.

Secondly, they exist for fellowship with other members of the team. We are meant to help, encourage and complement one another. No one person can give an adequate representation of what God is like, but together we can begin to give some pointers! This is our responsibility to one another.

Thirdly, the church exists to bear witness to Christ among those who do not yet know him, and to be of practical service in society. So public testimony to Jesus must be matched by a passion for justice and practical care for the neediest people in our midst. That is our responsibility to the world for which Christ died.

That is what we are for!

How can we experience the companionship of others on the journey?

I expect you are thinking I will be urging you to go to church. Wrong! The church is something we are, not somewhere we go to. Of course there must be times of coming together with other travellers on the road to experience being family, to praise and show our gratitude to God, to study the map, and maybe to hear from someone who understands it well, as well as to pray for the needs of the world and our community. That goes without saying. But it does not have to be in an ancient building in which we play a walk-on part in a dull drama led by people in funny clothes up front. Increasingly we are discovering new forms of being church. Sometimes folk gather in a pub or a restaurant. Sometimes they have been on an Alpha course exploring the meaning of life, and they want to stay together afterwards. Sometimes it is three or four surfers on the beach who belong to Jesus and are enjoying a Bible study together. We need to find the most appropriate form of companionship for ourselves, from which we can gain and to which we can contribute. And then we need to get stuck into that group or community, and become not an observer but a participant.

So make sure that your spirituality is shared with others who follow the same spiritual Guide. Let's have none of this stuff about 'I can be a Christian in my back garden. I don't need to meet with other Christians.' Yes you do! Don't kid yourself that 'My religion is my own affair.' If you sign on with Jesus Christ, it isn't! You become a soldier in his army, a stone in his temple, a member of his household, a child in his family, a branch in his tree. By definition, you are bonded with other followers of the Guide.

It was the great poet John Donne who reminded us that no man is an island: we are all part of the mainland. And that is vital for the Christian to remember. Sometimes we will be disappointed by fellow members of the church. There are perhaps some quarrelsome members in the family, some awkward stones in the building, some mutinous soldiers in the army! The trouble is, we are all very human and fallible. So while quite properly nourishing high expectations of our brothers and sisters in Christ, we also need to have a forgiving spirit – and to expect the same from them! Whatever the failures we may encounter in the Christian community, one thing is clear. Any spirituality that does not begin with the individual does not begin. But any spirituality that ends with the individual ends.

10

How Can I Get Some Discipline into My Spirituality?

This has been called the Age of Feeling. If it feels good, we go for it. On the whole, that applies to what we eat, what we wear, and the entertainments we choose. It tends to apply to our spirituality, too. If we are feeling enthusiastic, we might have an extended religious splurge, and then do nothing for another week or two. We probably realize that this is not ideal, but the problem is, how can we get some discipline into our spirituality without returning to the 'rule book' mentality of the past?

Discipline is not a popular idea these days, but the root of the word simply means 'learning'. The question resolves itself, therefore, into how we can learn from Jesus, the spiritual guide we have come to trust. Think of a high-quality tennis match – a Wimbledon final, perhaps. One of the players, after sailing through the first set, unaccountably loses his or her rhythm and makes a heap of unforced errors as a result. Sometimes the player manages to regain that rhythm before the end of the game, and it starts to flow again. Rhythm, it seems, is a key to success. It certainly is in the Christian life. How do we find a rhythm that will sustain us ? Here are a few suggestions.

Taking time with the guide

First, make sure that devotional time with the Lord is a regular feature in your life. I am afraid many Christians do not give God a chance. Indeed, they hardly spare him a thought, between one Sunday and the next. No wonder their spiritual lives are starved. Just as we need to take regular food if our bodies are to stay healthy, so we need to take regular spiritual food on board. We need to mark out some time in the day as special for re-establishing close links with Jesus. Most people find the early morning best for this, but for some night-owls that is the worst possible news! Find what time is best for you, but then stick to it. It was well known in the Eighth Army in North Africa in World War II that you did not disturb General Montgomery, commander of the British Forces, during a certain half hour each day upon any pretext whatever. He was talking to his God.

Sharing with colleagues

Secondly, remember that we are not intended to attempt to live the Christian life on our own. As we saw in the previous chapter, we are part of a community, limbs in a body, stones in a building. So we need to build a few regular communal points into our calendar, and stick to them. Church on Sunday could be one. A mid-week evening with your Christian group of friends might be another.

What's more, other people can help to keep us accountable. For example, if I was staying on my own in a foreign city, I might be tempted to go off to a sexy nightclub. But I would not do that if some of my Christian friends were with me. They would keep me on the straight and narrow without even realizing that they were doing so. So I fear for the 'My religion is my own affair' brigade. They do not allow themselves to be held accountable by friends who are, after all, trying to walk the same spiritual journey. We really do need some group to keep us accountable, and to meet with them on a regular basis. We are right to revel in our freedom: but freedom calls for accountability. At the end of the day, God will hold us accountable for the use we have made of our freedom.

Choosing a soul friend

Many Christians of a Catholic persuasion have found it a great help to have a 'spiritual director' whom they can meet with from time to time, to talk over their progress. In recent years many Christians of other traditions have come to see the value of this arrangement – albeit without great enthusiasm for the word 'director'! Perhaps 'soul friend' is a better description. At all events, it is someone with whom you can be totally honest about both the strengths and the weaknesses in your life, knowing that this discussion is in total confidence, and within an affirming and non-judgmental relationship. It is a bit like having an MOT for your car: checking to see what may not be functioning properly, and servicing what is doing well. You would find that meeting with a friend like this three or four times a year can be an enormous help in living a disciplined spiritual life.

Aiming for balance

We are hearing a lot these days about obesity and the danger it is to the nation's health. It comes, of course, from having too much food (or the wrong sort of food) and not enough exercise. We need to strike a proper balance. Physical obesity can affect our spiritual lives too. We are far less likely to be healthy, spiritually as well as physically, if we are grossly overweight. A proper balance of food, exercise and sleep does wonders for our spiritual as well as our physical health. I always find it rather sad when I see Christian leaders who are grossly obese and clearly have not maintained a good balance between their intake and their exercise. It sets a very poor example.

But there is a more spiritual aspect of this balance that I have in mind. We need to ensure that what we take in from God through the means we have outlined in previous chapters is kept in balance with what we give out to other people. God nourishes us not simply for our satisfaction but in order that we can be strong to help others.

In Israel there are two major inland seas. One is the Dead Sea. It has the River Jordan pouring into it all the time, but there is no outflow. It is rightly called 'dead'. The other is the Sea of Galilee, a beautiful bright lake, alive with fish and aquatic life. That too is fed by the Jordan. The difference between the two is just this. There is a proper balance between inflow and outflow in the Sea of Galilee, while the Dead Sea simply receives but never gives away. I do not want a spirituality like that, do you?

11

How Can I Develop a Spiritual World-view?

Everybody has a world-view – a way of looking at the world. The majority of us are not aware of it most of the time. It is like a pair of contact lenses through which we see everything, but of which we are rarely conscious. Some people's world-view is unashamedly hedonistic: how can I get the most pleasure for myself? For some, everything must be sacrificed for the sake of the family. Others see every aspect of life in the light of how it will affect their business and career. On the larger scale, it is obvious how communists and fascists have subordinated everything, including instincts of compassion, to their rigorous – and ruthless – world-views. Very well, then: how are spiritual people to develop a world-view that will reflect their priorities?

The sad thing to notice, to begin with, is that many Christians do not allow their faith to influence the way they live. They are to be seen in church on a Sunday, more or less regularly. But they do not seem to allow the ideals of the Man of Nazareth to affect their daily lives.

They have no greater concern for the environment than anyone else – but they should have if they really believe the Creator has made humankind the stewards of his creation. They are not notably more moral than anyone else – which they should be if they believe God has revealed standards of right and wrong and has given us his Holy Spirit to empower us to act rightly. Their marriages seem no more stable than other people's – and that, too, is odd if they believe that marriage is, for a Christian, the powerful and evocative image of the relationship between Christ and his church. Jesus himself spoke of those who would look but not perceive, and listen but not understand (Mark 4:12). How can we avoid being like them? What would an authentic spiritual world-view look like?

A view of the natural world

First, it would touch the area of the world around us. The believer does not see the natural world as something random and fortuitous, which is there to be enjoyed or raped according to the whim of human beings. He or she sees it as the product of divine creation, and therefore as something to be looked after and revered. A believer will not go overboard and worship Nature, but will worship the God who made the natural world and who discloses much of himself in that world. It was Albert Einstein who testified to his 'humble adoration of the illimitably superior Spirit who reveals himself in the slight details which we can perceive with our frail minds.' Or as J. S. Mill put it, 'Nature does testify to its Creator.' That is how the spiritual person will approach the natural world. He or she will revel in its beauty and seek to preserve it and look after it, and will also look through it, so to speak, in order to appreciate something of the divine self-disclosure in the natural world.

It was the great seventeenth-century English poet George Herbert who encouraged us to look at the natural world in this way. In his famous poem 'The Elixir' he says:

A man that looks on glass
On it may stay his eye;
Or if he pleaseth through it pass,
And then the heaven espy.

That is what the believer does. A window can be seen as a work of art in itself, especially if it is stained glass or highly decorated. We can easily focus our attention on it, but the window only serves its purpose when we look through it and see what lies beyond. Some people express this by taking what they call a 'sacramental' view of Nature. It is not an end in itself, but an accurate pointer to an underlying spiritual reality. I used to be almost a Gaia or Nature worshipper, lying out in the woods, inhaling the smells, watching the moles emerge from their underground corridors and the rabbits from their holes. But I can honestly say that since coming to Christ as my spiritual guide, I have enjoyed the natural world even more, because I know the one who made it, and it not only continues to enthral me but enhances my love for God and my understanding of him.

A view of human beings

The second main ingredient in a truly spiritual world-view is to see the people around us and people world-wide as created by God and, in some sense, made in his image – reflecting the personhood, values and life which are to be found in the divine nature. That 'image of the divine' is what gives to humans their dignity and value. Sadly, some who acknowledge God become religious fanatics and slaughter others: think of the medieval Crusades or the modern suicide bombers. That is bad enough. But if the concept of a superior spiritual force, which we call God, is removed from the picture, then people can be thought of as no more than sophisticated biological accidents. You may be very charming to them, as many atheists are. But you can with equal logic reckon that, since they have no intrinsic value, they can be wronged, or even killed, with impunity. The atheistic regimes of the twentieth century pursued that policy with ruthless efficiency. Between them Hitler, Stalin, Pol Pot and Mao liquidated hundreds of millions of people who did not fit in with their ideological world-view – a graphic and terrifying reminder that our world-view affects our politics.

By contrast, if we see the hungry, the abused, the ill-clothed, the dying as people made by God and of infinite value to him, that will arouse our compassion and our action. Maybe that will get us involved in contending for a just wage for impoverished workers, or fair trade with primary producing countries, or human rights in totalitarian regimes. The Christian Aid challenge is relevant: 'Live more simply that others may simply live.' It is very radical, this way of looking at human beings. There are enough resources in this world for every person's need, but not for every person's greed. And at present the West is obscenely greedy. We wallow in our affluence and get fixated on slimming, while 1.3 billion of the world's population live on less than a dollar a day and another 2 billion on less than two dollars a day. So a third of humankind subsists – or fails to – on a microscopic proportion of the world's wealth. Every day, 30,000 children die in Africa from diseases that are easily preventable with basic medicines. The trouble is – they lack them. A 1998 UN Human Development report showed that the three richest people in the world own wealth equal to the combined GDP of the world's poorest 48 countries. Did you know that basic education for the whole world would only cost an extra 6 billion dollars a year? Yet 8 billion are spent on cosmetics in the USA alone! If we are serious about developing a spiritual world-view, it is going to drive us to some pretty radical action. Christians should be, and indeed they are, in the forefront of the battle against ignorance, poverty and disease.

A view of morality

The third element in developing a spiritual world-view lies in the area of morality. Issues are increasingly complex in the world of stem-cell research and changing sexual mores. Often we are not asked to choose between black and white moral choices but rather between shades of grey. Our call is to go for the lightest shade. But how do we determine that? One way, which may not cover all questions but certainly covers most, is to ask ourselves what the supreme man of the spirit, Jesus Christ himself, would do if he were alive today and standing in our shoes. How would he respond to the situation presenting itself? For example, could you see Jesus performing a partial-birth abortion, where the infant is killed in the process of being born? (This happens in present-day America.) Could you see him buying cut-price bananas from growers who are well known to oppress their workforce? Would you see him buying cheap products from stores which give rock-bottom wages to their employees? Could you see him falsifying his income tax returns, if it would not be noticed?

There are more elements than these in developing an authentic spiritual world-view, but these three are paramount: the lens through which you view the natural world, human beings, and moral decisions. However far we have travelled along the path of the spirit, we all have a long way to go!

12

How Can I Cope with Pressures?

Pressures. We all have them. Nobody's life is a bed of roses, and the spiritual life emphatically is not. Jesus told his followers to expect temptations from within and persecution from without, and they have been the continuing experience of his followers down the ages.

Troubles

Many of our pressures arise from the sheer hassle of life. How is a young woman with four children, no husband and a small income, going to cope in today's society? The answer must be, on any showing – with difficulty. But as we have seen in the previous chapter, a third of the human race survives on less than two dollars a day, so it must be possible in a Western nation where there are various social safety-nets in place. Obviously, it is wise to find out what the local entitlements are, and then to claim them. That will make the sheer business of survival a bit easier.

But it will not remove the sense of strain. That is where the Christian community comes in. A woman in a situation like this may not be able to afford a baby-sitter, but a couple of teenage girls from the local church might be only too willing to come in and help for free on a regular basis, so as to give the mother some support. She might find a fellowship group invaluable not only in restoring her spiritual vitality but in finding friendship and practical assistance from others in the group. Many people find it a help to get together in a 'prayer triplet' with a couple of friends, to lay their problems before their Guide and claim his promise that 'where two or three are gathered together in my name, there am I in the midst of them.'

On any showing, it is vital to keep in touch with God through prayer. It is true, if a bit trite, that if we're too busy to pray, we're too busy. The apostle Paul lived a life of intense pressure, and his advice to the Christians at Philippi was as follows: 'Rejoice in the Lord always; again I will say, Rejoice ... The Lord is near. Do not worry about anything but in everything by prayer and supplication with thanksgiving let your requests be made known to God.' And then follows this marvellous promise: 'and the peace of God, which surpasses all understanding, will guard your hearts and your minds in Christ Jesus' (Philippians 4:4ff.). Notice that worrying is wrong, and we are not meant to do it. Instead we are to make our requests to God over anything and everything – not forgetting to thank him. And God's own peace, which surpasses our understanding (but, mercifully, not our experiencing), will set guard over our hearts with their feelings and our minds with their distressed thoughts, as we keep close to Jesus. Try it for size! I am confident you will see some remarkable answers to those worries when you lay them at his feet. And if you think that is idealistic, remember that these words were written by the apostle in a stinking prison when on trial for his life and watched over by a couple of sentries. If anyone had an excuse for worrying, he had.

Temptations

Quite a lot of the pressure on us arises not from the hustle and hassle of life, but from the temptations to which we are prone. Some of them are like old friends. We have been giving in to them for years. And now that we are trying to walk a spiritual path with Jesus Christ, they don't seem to diminish. If anything, they increase. Why should that be? The answer to that one is easy. A dead fish will float downstream, but a live fish will always face upstream against the current. And in the old days when we were spiritually dead, temptations were no great problem. We hardly noticed them. They were par for the course. But now that we are spiritually alive we notice them much more. We face them, and we would like to find a way to overcome them.

There are a few things to bear in mind as we look at this difficult area which affects us all. One is that temptation is not sin. Giving in to it is. There comes a point when, with our will, we say 'OK' to the temptation, and that is when it becomes wrong.

Secondly, everyone gets tempted: let's not kid

ourselves that it's worse for us than it is for anyone else. Jesus got tempted more than anyone, for the simple reason that he never once gave in to temptation, and so he had to face its full force in a way we can scarcely imagine – so often have we surrendered to it! (See Hebrews 4:15.) That's why he is in a unique position to help us.

Thirdly, God does not tempt anyone. That is Satan's speciality. But God allows it. Satan, the great enemy of souls, wants us to fail the test of the temptation. God, the great lover of souls, wants us to succeed in and through it, and so gain moral strength. And we are entrusted with the awesome decision whether we will go God's way, or the path down which his enemy seductively beckons us.

The really encouraging thing is that God, who calls us to a holy life, has also given us his Holy Spirit, who will give us inner strength if we ask for it – and not otherwise (1 Thessalonians 4:7–8). God is not in the business of forcing us to go his way. He loves, and he calls; what's more, he offers the strength of his Holy Spirit. But the choice is ours. You are on the victory side, the apostle John tells his readers, for 'Greater is he who is in you than he who is in the world' (1 John 4:4). He means that God's Holy Spirit, who has been implanted in the heart of the believer, is stronger than the anti-God forces he has been talking about which flourish in secular society. But we have to trust him for that power when the temptation first rears its head. So he returns to the topic in the next chapter and says, 'Whatever is born of God overcomes the world. And this is the victory that overcomes the world, our faith' (1 John 5:4).

You and I have a second birthday: when we entrusted our spiritual lives to Jesus Christ we were 'born of God', welcomed into his family, and we have the gift of the Spirit in our hearts. But still 'our faith' is needed if we are to overcome our temptations. We have to trust him for the strength he longs to give. Years ago I heard this wise insight into victory over temptation: 'I can't. He can. I can through him.' Fool that I am, I often fail to ask for that strength, or simply don't want it and determine to give in to the temptation. But I have known enough of that power, when I ask for it, to be absolutely sure it is both mighty and readily available.

Opposition

'All who want to live a godly life in Christ Jesus will be persecuted' (2 Timothy 3:12). That was the apostle Paul's conclusion as he lay in his cell awaiting execution for the 'crime' of following Jesus Christ in a world that did not. This remarkable man had to put up with enormous opposition once he had left the path of amassing spiritual brownie points through his religious observance, and began to walk the true spiritual path of companionship with Jesus. He certainly had more than his fair share of opposition. He occasionally recounts what following Christ had cost him: 'labours, imprisonments, countless floggings and often near death' (2 Corinthians 11:23). It is salutary to recall that in the last hundred years there have been more martyrdoms of Christians than in all the preceding centuries put together. In many parts of the world today, if you turn to Jesus, you may very well be killed. Jesus knew it would happen. If they hounded him to death for the shining brightness of his life, it would be the same with some of his followers.

People can only stand a limited amount of light: human beings generally prefer the dark or the shadows. 'People love darkness rather than light because their deeds are evil' (John 3:19). So do not be surprised if opposition comes your way. In the West it is not usually martyrdom. It may be merely the sneer: 'So you've gone religious, have you?' It may mean exclusion from some groups where we used to be welcome. It may mean losing our job because we are not prepared to lie. It may mean being cold-shouldered because we will not go with 'the boys' to see pornographic movies. Opposition comes in many forms, but it all springs from one source: unwillingness to walk the Jesus way, and a determination to make life difficult for those who do.

This is not easy to handle. But there are a few things that we can bear in mind that will help. First, Jesus has promised that he will never leave us nor forsake us (Hebrews 13:5). That is to say, he will never give us up and never let us down. That counts for a lot. Most Christians find that they are more than ever aware of the closeness of Jesus when they are under pressure.

Secondly, Christian companionship means a lot more when opposition strikes. We are drawn closer to those who share the same spiritual goals, for God does not intend us to suffer in isolation.

Thirdly, there is a reward for those who endure, and it is no bad thing to remember that when the pressure on us is particularly grim. Nobody should become a

Christian because of a selfish hope for heaven. But the assurance of heaven is a real help to Christians facing fierce opposition. Back to the apostle Paul in his cell awaiting death: 'From now on,' he writes, 'there is reserved for me a crown of righteousness, which the Lord, the righteous judge, will give me on that day – and not only to me, but also to all who have longed for his appearing' (2 Timothy 4:8). That includes you!

These are some of the ways that pressures crowd in upon us. They come to everyone. What matters is how we handle them. Will we allow them to be stumbling blocks for our spiritual lives – or will we make them stepping stones to a deeper spiritual walk with God?

13

How Can I Share My Spirituality with Others?

I f you have found treasure, it is only natural to want to share it. All the more so if that treasure is a relationship with the greatest spiritual guide the world has ever seen. In an age like ours, dominated by material values, many people are hungry for relationship. But they are very suspicious of organized religion in all its forms: the track record has not been attractive.

The big thing to realize is that while people are indeed allergic to religion in its recognizable forms, they still have a very real spiritual hunger. 'There's got to be more to life than this,' they say. The spiritual search is on, if only we can engage with it. I was reading only this morning about the response in 'sleepy' Devon to 'Just 10', a brilliantly conceived presentation of the ten commandments. The organizers were astounded by the thousands who crowded in, with traffic backing up to the motorway two and a half miles away. A local doctor, who was not a Christian, observed that most people these days were searching for a spirituality, but he thought that the church had completely missed it. How can we help friends who feel like this?

Some advice from the apostle Paul can help us here. He wrote asking the villagers in a place called Colossae to share in his spiritual outreach, while he lay in prison:

> Devote yourselves to prayer ... that God may open a door for our message ... for which I am in chains. Pray that I may proclaim it clearly, as I should. Be wise in the way you act towards outsiders, making the most of every opportunity. Let your conversation be always full of grace, seasoned with salt, so that you may know how to answer everyone.
>
> (Colossians 4:2–6)

Three complementary approaches are suggested here:

Our prayer

The most important way we can help anyone else to discover spiritual life is to pray for them. Nobody is willing to be told what to believe these days. They have got to find it for themselves if it is to be real. And it is not just a matter of their search. God has to make contact with them if there is to be any spiritual relationship. As Paul puts it, it is God who can 'open a door for our message'. So prayer is essential. Our words by themselves can never bring spiritual life. Only the Lifegiver can do that. So it is vital to pray to him about that friend whom we long to see 'come to life'.

Our lifestyle

People are rightly cynical about mere talk – especially from politicians and preachers. They are only going to be convinced by action or behaviour that they find arresting. Here Paul says our speech should be 'always full of grace' – that would be a change, wouldn't it? And it should be 'seasoned with salt'. Salt brings out the full flavour of our food and makes it attractive. If the way we spoke about others were always gracious and generous and winsome, it would predispose our friend to wonder how we managed it. And that would be the first step! Of course, it is not only our speech that matters. What we do is critical. If we are able to show a generosity, a remarkable level of self-sacrifice, that too may make our friend wonder at the spiritual resources we seem to have tapped into.

Our words

Sometimes people think that if we live a good life we do not need to say anything about our faith. None of the great religions would have taken off if their followers had adopted that approach! And anyhow, if I were to say nothing, a friend would be entitled to think I was just a nice person, rather than someone who had found a treasure he could never earn. We cannot afford to keep silent, if we want our friends to share in our discovery. There are three aspects of our conversation that Paul alludes to here.

The first is to give his testimony. He is not

embarrassed to say in this letter, written to these people he has never met, that the reason he is in prison is because he has put his trust in Christ. That personal testimony to the spirituality we have discovered carries a lot of weight. People are often intrigued by those three little words: 'I have found ...' Ours is an age of doubt, almost of cynicism. So to find someone humbly but joyfully saying that they have found a clear path in the spiritual jungle is inviting. Especially if the speaker is not a clergyman!

The second way is to explain clearly. That is not as difficult as you might think. Our friend is not satisfied spiritually: he knows he has not found a satisfactory basis for living, or he would not be asking for your help. He needs to admit he is not yet in touch with the God who made him – spirit, soul and body. So you need to explain to him that God loves him very much, wants his company, and even came to find him. What is more, God was prepared to take personal responsibility for the wrong stuff in his life, and in fact did so, once and for ever, on the cross. But he also smashed the power of death on Easter Day, and is alive and available. He invites your friend's allegiance. Ask him if he will give it. If he will, encourage him to pray a grateful, simple prayer, accepting God's welcome home. That will place his feet on the path of companionship with Christ, and get him started. If he is not yet ready to take such a step, that is where the third area of your speaking comes in.

The third way that Paul describes is, 'that you may know how to answer everyone'. In other words, you need to be able to give good reasons for choosing Christ rather than any other spiritual guide, and you need to know how to answer objections – this is what theologians call 'apologetics'. Naturally, skills like this do not grow overnight. It takes time and experience to answer the questions that people very properly raise. But we should aim to become increasingly competent at it.

Witness, explanation, apologetic. These are three sides of 'chattering' (the literal meaning of Paul's word 'proclaim') the good news. And it is very good news indeed – the best that human ears have ever heard. This should stimulate us to aspire to pass it on joyfully, naturally, modestly and clearly. The greatest service we can ever render anyone is to help them to find solid ground in their spiritual search.

14

How Can My Spirituality Help in My Suffering?

Suffering comes to all of us in some shape or form. It may be physical, mental or spiritual. None of us can escape it. It is one of the mysteries of our human existence.

Some people face it with a stiff upper lip. It is just one of those things we have to put up with. Not much comfort in that!

Others think it is God punishing them for something they have done in the past. But no. The Bible assures us that God does not willingly afflict the children of men.

Others get bitter – but that makes the whole thing worse.

What is the best way to handle suffering? Well, there are no easy answers. C. S. Lewis, the celebrated author of *The Lion, the Witch and the Wardrobe*, wrote a marvellous book called *The Problem of Pain*. But when his wife was dying, he found that the answers it gave failed to satisfy him. He wrote a much darker, but more personal book, *A Grief Observed*. Suffering is always grim, but the way we approach it is all-important.

The first thing that may help us is to remember that we worship a suffering God. He does not stay aloof from the human condition. He has come to share it. He did not live a charmed life devoid of suffering. He drained the cup of anguish to the dregs and endured the most awesome suffering anyone has ever had to put up with. In a word, there is nothing we can go through that he has not faced. There are no depths we may plumb where we can say to God, 'You don't understand.' However tough our circumstances, he can whisper, 'I do understand. I have been there too.' That does not remove the problem, but it makes it a little easier to bear.

The second thing that can help is to remember that, as the poet Keats put it, this world is 'a vale of soul making'. Anyone who understands the resurrection of Jesus can never accept that this world is all there is. If it were, suffering would be utterly senseless, obscene even. But if it is seen as a discipline, purifying us and preparing us for the life to come, it makes a bit more sense.

There's a third thing that helps a lot. The Lord has promised to be with us in all circumstances. In that famous twenty-third Psalm God undertakes to be our Shepherd and to stay with us even in the valley of the shadow of death. His companionship does not banish anguish, to be sure, but it can make it a little more bearable.

I guess what I am pleading for is that when we are going through a painful time, we should try to tread the path of partnership with our hand in the hand of a suffering God. I have met many people who have transformed their suffering in that way: 'I don't understand it ... but I trust you', has been their attitude.

We read in the Bible of a rich, godly man called Job who eventually arrived at that deep trust. But it took him 41 whole chapters to get there! Stripped of his possessions, covered with boils, bereaved of his family, this wretched man went through as tough a time as you could imagine. His friends gathered round him and offered him the conventional wisdom about suffering, which was useless to him. The chapters are full of barren arguments as these so-called friends piled guilt, criticism and sarcasm on top of his suffering, while Job vigorously defended himself. After shouting 'Why?' no less than sixteen times, Job had a deep encounter with God. Maybe his faith had been a bit second hand previously. At all events, now Job had an attitude of deep repentance and trust in God's love and provision. He was no longer seeking answers from God. He was enjoying relationship with God. Suffering can do that. It is rather like a fire which either softens or hardens, depending on what you put into it. The same fire that hardens clay softens wax. Shall we let our suffering harden and embitter us, or soften us? The choice is ours.

The cry we so often hear when suffering comes is, 'What have I done to deserve this?' And the answer is probably 'Nothing at all.' Suffering is not very often punishment (though it can be). It is much more often simply due to what it means to be human, with bodies and minds that can be injured, diseased and worn out.

Much suffering is inflicted by others – a stark reminder of humankind's capacity for evil as well as good.

The ultimate innocent sufferer was, of course, Jesus himself. He never did anything wrong, and yet he suffered as nobody ever had. He too cried out 'Why?' as he faced the ultimate struggle with the pain and evil of the world. There was no answer, except the grip of the Father's hand and the empathy of the Father's tears. Relationship was crucial for Jesus, as it had been for Job, and as it is for us. 'Into your hands I commend my spirit,' cried Jesus as he died.

Peter, that untrustworthy disciple who became such a man of rock, was no doubt skulking round that place of execution as Jesus died, and may well have heard what he said. He certainly got the message, which is so important for all of us who want our spirituality to hold fast in the face of suffering. This is what he wrote to fellow Christians suffering hardship: 'Let those who suffer in accordance with God's will do right, and commit themselves to a faithful Creator' (1 Peter 4:19).

15

How Can My Spirituality Help Me Face Death?

That really is the ultimate question, is it not? No philosophy, no spirituality is any good unless it can enable us to face death in a better frame of mind than what would have been possible without it. At the age of twenty we feel immortal. At forty we make sure that we have some life insurance. By sixty it is usual for our parents to have died and we realize we are next in line. And thereafter death becomes the reality we cannot avoid. Don't believe anyone who tells you that they are not afraid to die. We all shrink from it. As Rousseau put it: 'He who pretends to face death without fear is a liar.' It is surely much nearer the truth, as Dr Johnson bluntly affirmed, that 'no rational man can die without uneasy apprehension.' Why is this? Partly, of course, because we can hardly look forward with equanimity to the extinction of our life. But I wonder whether Epicurus, the Greek philosopher, was right when he gave this revealing answer: 'What men fear is not that death is annihilation, *but that it is not!*' W. B. Yeats, in his poem 'Death', makes much the same point:

> Nor dread nor hope attend
> A dying animal:
> A man awaits his end
> Dreading and hoping all.

There is no doubt, as T.S. Eliot once put it, that we seek 'distraction, delusion, escape into dreams, pretence' when the topic of death comes up. It is the unmentionable subject of the twenty-first century, like sex was in the nineteenth. It's the thing that always happens to someone else.

How then, can our Christian spirituality help us face the 'last enemy'? The answer lies fairly and squarely in the resurrection of Jesus Christ from the dead. The empty tomb, the resurrection appearances, the launch of the church, the conversion of enemies like Saul of Tarsus, the transformation of people's lives from that day to this, the change of the day of rest from Saturday to Sunday – all of these undeniable facts validate the claim of many historians that the resurrection is the best-attested fact in history. Very well. If that is so, just think what the resurrection of Jesus means.

First, it confirms his claim to be the supreme spiritual guide. No other spiritual leader has risen from the chill of the grave. The tomb of Mohammed in Medina contains the bones of the prophet, who is very dead. No tomb contains the bones of Jesus, who is very much alive. That sets him in a different league from all the other spiritual leaders of humankind.

Secondly, it means that he decisively defeated the power of death. As C. S. Lewis put it: 'he has forced open a door that had been locked since the death of the first man. He has met, fought, and beaten the King of Death. Everything is different because he has done so. This is the beginning of the New Creation. A new chapter in cosmic history has opened.'

Thirdly, his resurrection offers us a new and solid hope in the face of death. He had promised his followers on the last night of his life that he was going before them to prepare a welcome in the Father's home. A wonderful promise – but could it be trusted? It could not be denied once Jesus was raised from the grave to the power of an endless life. When we die we shall go to be for ever with the one who has guided us through life.

Fourthly, his resurrection affects the way we mourn the loss of our loved ones. The Bible tells us: 'We do not want you to be uninformed about those who have died, so that you may not grieve as others do, who have no hope' (1 Thessalonians 4:13ff.). Of course we shall mourn them, but not with the bitter intensity and hopelessness of those who know nothing of the resurrection hope brought by Jesus. Our Christian dead are with the Risen One. They are already more alive than we are.

What will that resurrection life be like? We cannot know, for death erects a great curtain, and we cannot see what is happening the other side of it. But the apostle Paul once again comes to our aid with two marvellous hints. When writing to Christians at Corinth about death and its sequel, he calls Jesus' resurrection the 'first-fruits of the dead'. And where there is a first-fruit there is a main crop to come. Those who love him and follow him will be part of it. We will possess a 'spiritual body' (1 Corinthians 15:44) like Jesus did after the resurrection. We will be recognizably ourselves, but no longer subject to the limitations of our physical bodies.

The other hint he gives us is from agriculture. Just suppose you had lived in the inner city all your life, and had never seen a field of corn. You would be astonished to learn that the little grain of wheat which somebody dropped into your hand could be transformed into a tall plant with leaves and a full ear, and could become part of that glorious wheat field. Well, that is the illustration Paul gives of the transformation that will happen in the lives of believers after their death (see 1 Corinthians 15).

What a brilliant analogy! The fully grown plant contains the same life that you put into the ground as a seed that would die: but that transformed life has far greater possibilities now, far greater splendour than you could have imagined when it was a bare little grain. That's the measure by which our resurrection life will exceed our present one. That is something wonderful to look forward to. No wonder the apostle Paul ends his chapter on resurrection in 1 Corinthians with a triumphant cry, echoing the hopes of the Old Testament believers: 'Death has been swallowed up in victory.'

So I, for one, am looking forward to being dead: it will mean 'to be with Christ which is far better' (Philippians 1:23). But I am not looking forward to the process of dying, which is often painful and lengthy.

Even here, however, we are offered help. Our Guide has promised that he will be with us to the very end, and that nothing in life or death can separate us from his companionship and his love (Matthew 28:20; Romans 8:38–39). Paul envisages the possibility of Christians being slaughtered like sheep, but because of the companionship of Jesus he can cry out in the same breath: 'No, in all these things we are more than conquerors through him who loved us' (Romans 8:37).

What other spiritual guide can offer anything comparable in the face of death? I don't know one. Do you?

16

Taste and See!

A few years ago I was invited to speak at a Christian meeting in the village pub. It began as a beer-tasting competition, hosted by the vicar. Everyone was given samples of six different kinds of beer, and we each had to name the brands. Only one person among the fifty regulars present got them all right!

How was I to speak in such a situation? I decided that the appropriate approach was to invite everyone to exercise their spiritual taste buds. I spoke on this invitation from the Psalms: 'Taste and see that the Lord is good. Happy is the person who puts his trust in him' (Psalm 34:8). What followed the talk was remarkable. Conversations on spiritual things broke out all over that pub, and continued long after closing time.

We all want to be happy. If our chosen brand of spirituality does not make us happy, it is not much good. All of us know we have to make choices, and we live with the consequences. In the spiritual realm, is there any sense in playing a hunch, making a blind guess, like the beer-tasters did that night? Surely not. We need to make an informed decision on the spirituality we choose. It has to be solidly based, and it has to be relevant to every aspect of our lives.

In this short, introductory book I have tried to lay out why the best place to start our search for spiritual reality is the one who claimed to bring God onto the stage of human life. Nobody else has claimed that, let alone backed it as Jesus did with a matchless life, peerless teaching, staggering claims, the most famous death in the world and resurrection to new life. If you should find him unsatisfactory, then by all means turn to the hundreds of other spiritual options. But there is only one spiritual leader who claims to embody God, and his name is Jesus. It is only sensible, then, to start our exploration into spirituality by examining Jesus: what he claims, what he offers and what he achieved. That is what I have tried to do in this little book. I wanted to give an outline, a bird's-eye view, of a spirituality that will sustain you throughout this life and beyond.

We have seen that the resurrection is absolutely crucial to the Christian message, and that it is very strongly attested. It really is the lynchpin of the whole case for Jesus. I encourage you to examine the evidence with care if you are in doubt about it. It will bear the most critical scrutiny.

But consider the consequences if Jesus really is the Son of God and has genuinely risen victorious over death. He can be the guide I need, since he has been this way before. He can offer me the forgiveness I need, since his resurrection validates what he did on the cross. He can guide me with the map of his Scriptures, feed me with the meal he instituted, bind me together with other friends of his, and relate to me in prayer and contemplation. The most awesome thing is that this Jesus, who is still very much alive and well today, is willing to come and enter our lives if we will have him. That is what the word 'Christian' indicates – Christ in me! Of course, this is not a physical indwelling. It is what he longs to do through his unseen Holy Spirit. And if we welcome him into our very being, of course there will be some victories over the old temptations. Of course there will be a new love for others, reflecting the love that Jesus had for others in the days when he walked the roads of Palestine. And of course he can sustain us in our rough times and hold our hand as we face up to death. And then he will take us home.

It is a marvellous scenario. It is rooted in history, it is coherent, and it makes sense. That is what the living God wants to do with you and me – to come on board and bring our spirituality to life.

At present I guess you are spiritually hungry, or you would not be reading this book. He wants to satisfy that hunger and give you joy and fulfilment. He wants to clean you up, make you useful in a broken world, and at the end of the day, welcome you face to face in heaven. You will never find an offer that is remotely comparable, however long you search among the religions and spiritual practices of the world. Jesus, and his willingness to come and share our lives, stands head and shoulders above any of the other spiritual leaders on offer. And he has proved his trustworthiness through centuries of transforming the lives of men and women.

But here's the point. There is no way he can do this for you and me unless we offer him access to our lives. He cannot clean up and refit the house of your life while standing outside the door. And I should hate you to finish this little book and think, 'That was quite interesting', but fail to take the decisive step that would allow you to taste and see for yourself that the Lord is good.

We have already looked at that step in Chapter 4. We spoke of joining up, of starting out on the path. But just possibly you skimmed over that bit and did nothing about it. Please think again. The image we are now considering is one of tasting. You can never *see* if the Lord is good until you *taste*. That requires a definite act on your part. Tasting is about as basic as any action gets. You are thirsty. You believe the drink will do you good. But you have to taste if you are going to find out.

I remember well the day I 'tasted'. The image that my friend used with me that day was different yet again. Not joining up, not tasting, but opening up. A different analogy, but the same need to receive Jesus' offer if I was to enjoy what he wanted to give me. My friend showed me a verse in the Bible that I had never seen before. Jesus was speaking. He said: 'Be earnest, and repent. Listen! I am standing at the door, knocking; if you hear my voice and open the door I will come in to you and eat with you, and you with me' (Revelation 3:20). It was a very clear picture. It showed me that Jesus was standing outside the door of my life, and amazingly, he wanted to come in. I needed to repent of my long-standing attitude which had kept him out. I needed humbly to ask him in. And I did, one Sunday afternoon in a sports pavilion. With that act of commitment I began to taste and see for myself that the Lord is good.

Of course, that was only the (essential) beginning of a relationship that has developed over the years. Perhaps you have already taken that step, but have set aside no regular time for meeting with your Spiritual Guide. Your Bible gathers dust, and prayer is sketchy at best. That needs to change. Taste and see that the Lord is good!

I meet an increasing number of people these days who are disillusioned with the church and accordingly cut themselves off from Christian fellowship. Perhaps you are one of them. You need that companionship of fellow believers. You are part of God's family. You need to meet others round the family table. Taste and see that the Lord is good!

Have you, perhaps, begun, but have never got any discipline into your spiritual life? You will find it flows much better when there is some rhythm to it. Try it for a month, and I am confident you will agree. Taste and see!

This morning in my time of meeting with my Guide, it so happened that I was reading 1 Peter chapter 2. I was struck by the way Peter had picked up the 'Taste and see' theme from Psalm 34. Listen to his desire for his readers: 'Like newborn infants, long for the pure spiritual milk, so that by it you may grow into salvation – if indeed you have tasted that the Lord is good' (1 Peter 2:2–3).

That would be his desire for you and me, as well. It would be such a shame to miss it!